UNIFORM CIVIL CODE – UNDER ARTICLE 44 OF INDIAN CONSTITUTION

VOLUME 2, ISSUE 3 OF BRILLOPEDIA

ADITHYA NARAYANAN

Contents

Preface

"Start writing, no matter what. The water does not flow until the faucet is turned on".

- Louis L'Amour

Hundreds of students and professors are contributing their work to Brillopedia, we are here to provide ample information about Law and Contemporary issues. Our aim is to provide a platform for today's generation to express their views and ideas on law and contemporary law.

Author

Adithya Narayanan

Publication

This research paper is published in volume 2, issue 3 of Brillopedia

CHAPTER ONE

ABSTRACT

The Uniform Civil Code (UCC), necessitates for the establishment of one law for India, that is applicable to all religious groups in affairs such as marriage, divorce, inheritance, adoption. The code falls under Article 44 of the Indian Constitution, which formulates that the state be obliged to aim to secure UCC for the citizens all over the country India.

The topic of the UCC has appeared into India's political discussion recently, because of several Muslim women, affected resentfully by the personal laws, have set about tapping the doors of the Supreme Court to endorse their fundamental rights to liberty and equality in maintaining with constitutional provisions.

Recently the union law ministry demanded the law commission to inspect the affairs in connection with the application of Uniform Civil Code.

Uniform Civil Code, fundamentally and literally denotes one nation one law, legally the word Civil Code means to balance the whole body of laws controlling rights associating to property and if not in personal affairs like marriage, divorce, maintenance, adoption and inheritance. Uniform Civil Code actually means merging all these, "personal law" to have one set of secular laws dealing with these features that are bound to apply to all citizens of India regardless of the community they belong to, nevertheless an exact amount has not been depicted yet, but however the exact form of such a Uniform Code have not been defined, it must probably be included in most modern and developing features of all subsisting personal laws, while rejecting those which are regressive. Primarily Uniform Code is a attempt to provide the full image a more balanced and structured.

Thus, this article discusses on the needs, origin, pros and cons of Uniform Civil Code in India.

INTRODUCTION

Uniform Civil Code in India advances to restore the personal laws based on the scriptures and customs of each paramount religious group in the country with prevalent set governing each and every citizen.

The Constitution of India, provides for Uniform Civil Code under **Article 44 as a Directive Principle of State Policy,** which expresses that, "The State shall endeavor to secure for the citizens a Uniform Civil Code throughout the territory of India.

CHAPTER THREE

NEED FOR UNIFORM CIVIL CODE

The political party namely Bharathiya Janatha Party propagates the implementation of uniform civil code, but the other political parties are against the implementation of the Uniform Civil Code.

The specific object of the Uniform Civil Code is to homogenize the personal laws of all religions. In other words, India should have a uniform law dealing with marriage, divorce, succession, inheritance and maintenance of all religions.

In the case of **Mohammad Ahmed Khan Vs. Shah Bano Begum** popularly known as the **Shah Bano case,** the then **Chief Justice of India, Y.V. Chandrachud** observed, "A common civil code will help the cause of national integration by removing disparate loyalties to law which have conflicting ideologies."

However, the then Congress government was of the view that there should be no interference with the personal laws, unless the demand comes from within the religions.[1]

Justice Kuldip Singh opined, "where more then 80 percent of the citizens have already been brought under the codified personal law, there is no justification whatsoever to keep in abeyance, any more, the introduction of the '**Uniform Civil Code'** for all the citizens in the territory of India."

Chief Justice Khare states "we would like to state that Article 44 provides that the State shall endeavor to secure for all citizens a uniform civil code throughout the territory of India.

It is now a matter of great regret that **Article 44 of the Constitution** has not been given effect to. Parliament is still to step in for framing a common civil code in the country. A common civil code will help the cause of national integration by removing the contradictions based on ideologies."

Thus,**the apex court** has on several instances directed the government to realize the directive principle enshrined in our Constitution and the urgency to bring in a uniform civil code. It is evident from the above observations of the judiciary that the responsibility lies on the State to have a uniform civil code for better governance of the state.

Justice R.M. Sahai observes that a unified code is imperative, both, for protection of the oppressed and for promotion of national unity and solidarity.

UCC should be a code, which is just and proper according to a man of ordinary prudence, without any bias with regard to religious or political considerations.

Despite knowing the advantages of having a uniform civil code, the political parties aiming at the vote bank of the minority communities, have not taken real steps to bring consensus among the various communities and in a legislation for a uniform civil code.

- The State should preserve and improve animal husbandry and prohibit slaughter of cows and calves.
- Forests and wildlife of the country should be protected through enactment of strict laws.
- The State should protect every monument or places of objects of historic interest.
- In order to promote the rule of law, the State should separate them judiciary from the executive.
- The State should promote international peace, maintain honorable relations between nations, and encourage settlement of international disputes by arbitration.

[1]Shubhra Anand Jain, *Uniform Civil Code*, UCC Full Form, Article 44 Uniform Civil Code https://byjusexamprep.com/uniform-civil-code-ucc-i.

CHAPTER FOUR

GENESIS OF UNIFORM CIVIL CODE

The birth of Uniform Civil Code precedes to colonial India, when the British Government put forward its report on 1835 emphasizing the need for consistency in the codification of Indian Law correlating with evidence, crime and contracts, especially endorsing those personal laws of Hindus and Muslims be retained outside such codification.[1]

Rise in legislations, dealing with personal problems in the backside of the British rule pressurized the government to form the B.N. Rau committee to codify Hindu law in 1941. The duty of the Hindu law committee was to inquire the necessity of common Hindu laws. The committee, in line with scriptures, suggested a civil code of marriage and succession for Hindu law, which could give equal rights to females. The 1937 act was analyzed and the committee endorsed a civil code of marriage and succession for Hindus.

Thus, all over the country, there was a disparity in liking for scriptural or customary laws since in several Hindu and Muslim communities, these were from time to time at dispute, such cases were present in community like the Dravidians and Jats. The Hindu law got preference due to their comparative ease in its execution, liking for such a system by both British as well as Indian judges and their agitation of hostility from the high caste Hindus. The struggle in exploring each particular practice of any community, created customary laws to come into effect with regard to the end of 19th century, recommending local opinion, the acceptance of individual customs arose.

[1]*What is Uniform Civil Code, Article 44 Importance, Hindu Code Bill, Business Standard* https://www.business-standard.com/about/what-is-uniform-civil-code.

CHAPTER FIVE

ADVANTAGES OF UNIFORM CIVIL CODE

1. To furnish equivalent status to all citizens

In the present-day era, a temporal democratic republic must have a common civil and personal laws for its citizen regardless of their religion, class, caste, gender, etc.

2. To encourage gender equality

It is frequently observed that personal laws of practically all religions are prejudiced towards women. Men are generally accorded with upper preferential status in circumstances of succession and inheritance. Uniform Civil Code will lead both men and women equally.[1]

3. To assist the desires of the youth

The present-day India is a entirely new public with 55% of its people is lower than 25 years of age. Their social frame of mind and desires are made by comprehensive and worldwide theories of equality, man kind and modernity. Their outlook of discharging identity on the basis of any religion has to be given a significant deliberation so, as to make use of full prospects towards nation establishment.

4. To keep-up with national integration

Before the court of law, all Indian citizens are equal as the criminal laws and other civil laws excluding personal laws, are same for all. With the execution of Uniform Civil Code, all natives will share the one and the same set of personal laws. There will be no extent of institutionalization of matters of the discrimination or compromise or particular advantages benefitted particular community on the basis of their specific religious personal laws.

5. **To go round the controversial problems for improvement of existing personal laws**

Existing personal laws are mostly based on the upper- class forbearing notions of the public in all religion. The call for UCC is usually made by resentful women as a relief for existing personal laws as patriarchal orthodox people consider the reforms in personal laws will demolish their sanctity and argue it abundantly.

[1]https://www.iassolution.com/uniform-civil-code-advantages-and-disadvantages/.

CHAPTER SIX

DISADVANTAGES OF UNIFORM CIVIL CODE

1. Possible troubles due to diversity in India

It is possibly difficult to come up with a usual and uniform set of rules for personal problems like marriage because of huge cultural diversity in India over the religions, states, sects, castes, etc.

2. Approach of Uniform Civil Code as intrusion into religious freedom

Numerous communities, especially minority community, views UCC as an intrusion into their rights of religious freedom. They agitate that a common code will deteriorate their traditions and inflict rules which will be mostly demanded and determined by the major part of religious community.

3. Intervention of state in personal affairs

The Indian Constitution furnishes for the right to freedom of religion of one's choice. With allocation of uniform rules and its pressure, the purview of the freedom of religion will be decreased.

4. Subtle and firm task

In its true spirit, such a code, is to be put forward by taking freely from different personal laws, making continuous changes in each, providing judicial declaration, promising gender equality and acquiring extensive interpretation on marriage, adoption, maintenance and succession by granting the profits that one community affixed from the others. This job will be very challenging time and human resource wise. The government must be tactful and impartial at each step while treating with the minority and majority communities. Or else, it might transpire to be more destructive in a form of anarchy.

5. Reform cannot be enforced due to unsuitable time

Observing a crucial disparity from Muslim community in India under this matter overlying with disputes over beef, saffronization of school and college curriculum, love jihad, and the quietness emerging from the top leadership on these disputes, there requires to be provided with ample towards common will become futile leaving minority class specifically Muslims further insecure and at risk to get influenced towards fanatic and reactionary ideas.[1]

[1]*The Pros and Cons of a Uniform Civil Code*, Eat My News (Sept. 25, 2019), https://www.eatmy.news/2019/09/what-is-uniform-civil-code.html.

CHAPTER SEVEN

CONCLUSION

Therefore, a Uniform Civil Code at most can come out from end to end of a developmental process, which maintain India's rich legal heritage, of which all the personal laws are equal elements. The multiple democracy is recognized by the present-day India. Thus, attempts must be directed on consonance in multiplicity than blanket consistency for prospering Indian economy.